HERE
THERE BE
ANGELS

Jane Yolen

HERE THERE BE ANGELS

Illustrated by DAVID WILGUS

HARCOURT BRACE & COMPANY

San Diego   New York   London

"Once a Good Man" by Jane Yolen previously appeared in *The Hundredth Dove and
Other Tales*, copyright © 1977 by Jane Yolen, published by T. Y. Crowell. "Angelica" by
Jane Yolen first appeared in *The Magazine of Fantasy and Science Fiction*, copyright © 1979 by
Jane Yolen. "The Boy Who Had Wings" copyright © 1974 by Jane Yolen, published by
T. Y. Crowell. "Brother Kenan's Bell" by Jane Yolen previously appeared in *Tales of Wonder*,
copyright © 1983 by Jane Yolen, published by Schocken Books. All reprinted by
permission of the author's agent, Curtis Brown, Ltd.

Library of Congress Cataloging-in-Publication Data
Yolen, Jane.
Here there be angels/Jane Yolen; illustrated by David Wilgus.
p.   cm.
Summary: An illustrated collection of the author's stories and poems about angels.
ISBN 0-15-200938-8
1. Angels—Literary collections.   [1. Angels—Literary collections.]
I. Wilgus, David, ill.   II. Title.
PZ7.Y78Hf   1996   95-48789

Designed by Camilla Filancia and Linda Lockowitz
First edition   F E D C B A

Printed in the United States of America

To Dick and Liz Stemple

in memory of the angel

in the garden at Culross

Contents

HERE
THERE BE
ANGELS

For three years Nancy Willard and I wrote angel poems back and forth to one another. We had discovered a mutual interest in angelic lore and thought we might do a book together. That book—Among Angels—turned out to be for adults, and so we dropped the younger poems from the collection.

This poem is one I originally sent to Nancy in answer to a poem of hers called "A Count of Angels."

Another Count of Angels

Angels at my heart and head
Keep imagination fed.

And at each shoulder, two,
One red, one blue,
To tell my stories to.

An angel at front door and back,
One for art and one for fact:
For story and for poetry.
And one for song. Angels three.

Four angels by my chair.
Four angels 'round my hair.
*Two to watch and two to pray
And one to bear my soul away.*

When I was twelve years old, I went to summer camp in Vermont. Camp Indianbrook. It was—still is—a Quaker camp, and we began every morning with Quaker meeting, sitting quietly, thinking or meditating. But because we were young—and most of us were not Quakers—the camp leaders, Susan and Ken Webb, started the silent meeting by reading or telling us a story so we would have something to think about. One day they told an old folktale that dealt with the difference between Heaven and Hell. I did not remember it word for word. But the essence of the story stuck with me, and about twenty-five years later I wrote "Once a Good Man."

I have since discovered that a number of versions of this tale exist, including a rabbinical story in which long silver spoons are used, and a Chinese version in which the implements for eating are chopsticks.

My version has been told in churches, synagogues, schools, and libraries, which, of course, delights me.

Once a Good Man

Once a good man lived at the foot of a mountain. He helped those who needed it and those who did not. And he never asked for a thing in return.

Now it happened that one day the Lord was looking over his records with his Chief Angel and came upon the Good Man's name.

"*That* is a good man," said the Lord. "What can we do to reward him? Go down and find out."

The Chief Angel, who was nibbling on a thin cracker, swallowed hastily and wiped her mouth with the edge of her robe.

"Done," she said.

So the Chief Angel flew down, the wind feathering her wings, and landed at the foot of the mountain.

"Come in," said the man, who was not surprised to see her. For in those days angels often walked on Earth. "Come in and drink some tea. You must be aweary of flying."

And indeed the angel was. So she went into the Good Man's house, folded her wings carefully so as not to knock the furniture about, and sat down for a cup of tea.

While they were drinking their tea, the angel said, "You have led such an exemplary life, the Lord of Hosts has decided to reward you. Is there anything in the world that you wish?"

The Good Man thought a bit. "Now that you mention it," he said, "there is one thing."

"Name it," said the angel. "To name it is to make it yours."

The Good Man looked slightly embarrassed. He leaned over the table and said quietly to the angel, "If only I could see both Heaven and Hell I would be completely happy."

The Chief Angel choked a bit, but she managed to smile nonetheless. "Done," she said, and finished her tea. Then she stood up and held out her hand.

"Hold fast," she said. "And never lack courage."

So the Good Man held fast. But he kept his eyes closed all the way. And before he could open them again, the man and the angel had flown down, down, down, past moles and mole hills, past buried treasure, past coal in seams, past layer upon layer of the world, till they came at last to the entrance to Hell.

The Good Man felt a cool breeze upon his lids and opened his eyes.

"Welcome to Hell," said the Chief Angel.

The Good Man stood amazed. Instead of flames and fire, instead of mud and mire, he saw long sweeping green meadows edged around with trees. He saw long wooden tables piled high with food. He saw

3

chickens and roasts, fruits and salads, sweetmeats and sweet breads, and goblets of wine.

Yet the people who sat at the table were thin and pale. They devoured the food only with their eyes.

"Angel, O angel," cried the Good Man, "why are they hungry? Why do they not eat?"

And at his voice, the people all set up a loud wail.

The Chief Angel signaled him closer.

And this is what he saw: The people of Hell were bound fast to their chairs with bands of steel. There were sleeves of steel from their wrists to their shoulders. And though the tables were piled high with food, the people were starving. There was no way they could bend their arms to lift the food to their mouths.

The Good Man wept and hid his face. "Enough!" he cried.

So the Chief Angel held out her hand. "Hold fast," she said. "And never lack courage."

So the Good Man held fast. But he kept his eyes closed all the way. And before he could open them again, the man and the angel had flown up, up, up, past eagles in their eyries, past the plump clouds, past the streams of the sun, past layer upon layer of sky, till they came at last to the entrance to Heaven.

The Good Man felt a warm breeze upon his lids and opened his eyes.

"Welcome to Heaven," said the Chief Angel.

The Good Man stood amazed. Instead of clouds and choirs, instead of robes and rainbows, he saw long sweeping green meadows edged around with trees. He saw long wooden tables piled high with food. He saw chickens and roasts, fruits and salads, sweetmeats and sweet breads, and goblets of wine.

But the people of Heaven were bound fast to their chairs with bands of steel. There were sleeves of steel from their wrists to their

5

shoulders. There seemed no way they could bend their arms to lift the food to their mouths.

Yet these people were well fed. They laughed and talked and sang praises to their host, the Lord of Hosts.

"I do not understand," said the Good Man. "It is the same as Hell, yet it is not the same. What is the difference?"

The Chief Angel signaled him closer.

And this is what he saw: Each person reached out with his steel-banded arm to take a piece of food from the plate. Then he reached over—and fed his neighbor.

When he saw this, the Good Man was completely happy.

Back in college I wrote the first version of this poem after taking a course in Russian history and learning about Peter the Great, the czar who tried to westernize Russia. Among other innovations, Peter the Great insisted that his nobles shave their beards.

Saint Peter guards the gates of Heaven in many traditional stories. I thought a meeting between these two Peters might strike some interesting sparks.

A Tale of Two Peters

Winging toward the golden doors
Of tradition-bound Heaven,
Where Pete at the gate lets in
White-horsed heroes,
The westernized soul of Peter the Great
(who let there be light and there was)
Came clean shaven.

He noted with great regret
The saintly beard
Whitening the guardian's chin,
The choir of constant angels
Singing old inspired hymns
Of a birth so awe-surrounded
Reason failed to credit it.

He noted with great regret
The ancient throne
Unlined by time's antiquing passage,
Stable since birth.

Peter sighed and shook his head:
The waste of power,
The lack of new creation.

"Down below," he mused quietly,
"Change and growth
Like hothouses force new flowerings.
But we must start where we are,
Eliminating superstition."
"I'll lose my job!" cried the saintly doorman.
"Sounds reasonable," said Peter.

Two British writers—Rob Meade and David Wake—invented the Drabble Project. They asked one hundred writers to each create a fantasy or science fiction story of exactly one hundred words. (The title doesn't count.) I was one of the authors in the second volume, with a dragon story. But I enjoyed doing it so much I wrote an angel story the same way.

Willa (named for my friend Willa Perlman) sees the kind of angel mentioned in the Old Testament. Marcus sees a Christian angel. And Fatima's angel is one of the many Hindu angels. One hundred multicultural words!

The School Visitor

The school visitor spoke to the class. "How many of you have seen an angel?"

Willa said, "In my garden was a tall man with four wings."

Marcus raised his hand. "I saw one in the kitchen, singing, 'Onward Christian soldiers . . .'"

Fatima was silent, smiling shyly. At last she offered, "I saw a *gandharva* playing his sitar. The music was heavenly."

One by one the children told their tales.

When class was over, the school visitor thanked the teacher. Then, pumping his mighty wings, white-feathered, tinged with apricot—he rose into the air.

The teacher did not see him go.

After Meade and Wake finished their hundred-word project, the American science fiction fan publisher Ed Meskys decided to publish a book of fifty-word stories. Again, the titles didn't count. I wrote a dragon story for Ed as well.

Writing a story in fifty words can be quite a challenge. This angel fifty-worder derives from the famous biblical story of Jacob's Ladder.

Jacob's Ladder

Jacob stood at the foot of a tall ladder that reached all the way to heaven. There were angels on every rung.

Jacob counted: *One. Two. Three . . .* "Look!" he cried out to a passing rabbi. "Angels are climbing up the ladder."

"Perhaps they are descending," said the wise old man.

My father's family came from Ykaterinislav, a small town near Kiev in the Ukraine. Like the villagers in this story, my father's family was Jewish by custom and culture but not particularly religious. My father did become a writer—a newspaperman and public relations expert—which means he was a kind of storyteller. But he's not the boy in this story. I have written a book about my family in the old country, called And Twelve Chinese Acrobats.

The description of the Angel of Death is mostly biblical (from Ezekiel) and the core story is a variant of an old tale that has been told variously about King David and about the famous rabbi Reb Lowe. Metatron, according to the Cabala, is the highest of all the angels. He has many other names.

The House of Seven Angels

My grandparents lived in the Ukraine in a village known as Ykaterinislav. It was a sleepy little Jewish town near Kiev, but if you go to look for it now, it is gone.

The people there were all hardworking farmers and tradesfolk, though there was at least one poor scholar who taught in the heder, a rabbi with the thinnest beard imaginable and eyes that leaked pink water whenever he spoke.

These were good people, you understand, but not exactly religious. That is, they went to shul and they did no work on the Sabbath and they fasted on Yom Kippur. But that was because their mothers and fathers had done so before them. Ykaterinislav was not a place that took to change. But the people there were no more tuned to God's note than any other small village. They were, you might say, tone-deaf to the cosmos.

Like most people.

And then one autumn day in 1897—about ten years before my

grandparents even began to think about moving to America—a wandering rabbi came into the village. His name was Reb Jehudah and he was a very religious man. Some even said that he was the prophet Elijah, but that was later.

Reb Jehudah studied the Torah all day long and all night long. He put all the men in Ykaterinislav to shame. So they avoided him. My grandfather did, too, but he took out his books again, which had been stored away under the big double bed he and Grandma Manya shared. Took them out but never quite got around to reading them.

And then one of the village children, a boy named Moishe, peeked into Reb Jehudah's window. At first it was just curiosity. A boy, a window, what else could it have been? He saw the reb at dinner, his books before him. And he was being served, Moishe said, by seven angels.

Who could believe such a thing? Though the number, seven, was so specific. So the village elders asked the boy: How did he know they were angels?

"They had wings," Moishe said. "Four wings each. And they shone like brass."

"Who shone?" asked the elders. "The angels or the wings?"

"Yes," said Moishe, his eyes glowing.

Who could quarrel with a description like that?

Of course the village men went to visit Reb Jehudah to confirm what Moishe had seen. But they saw no angels, with or without wings. Like Balaam of the Bible, they had not the proper eyes.

But for a boy like Moishe to have been given such a vision . . . this was not the kind of rascal who made up stories. Indeed, Moishe was, if anything, a bit slow. Besides, such things had been known to happen, though never before in Ykaterinislav.

And so the elders went back to Butcher Kalman's house for tea, to discuss this. And perhaps Butcher Kalman put a bit of schnapps in

15

their cups. Who can say? But they talked about it for hours—about the possibility of angels in Ykaterinislav, and in the autumn, too.

It was *pilpul,* of course, argument for argument's sake, even if they quoted Scripture. After a while, though, their old habits of nonbelief reclaimed them and they returned to their own work, but with renewed vigor. The crops, the shops, even the heder were the better for all the talk, so perhaps the angels were good for something after all.

Reb Jehudah knew nothing of this, of course. He continued his studying, day and night, night and day, wrestling with the great and small meanings of the law.

Now, one day an eighth angel came to visit him, an angel dressed in a long black robe that had pictures of eyes sewn into it, eyes that opened and closed at will. There was a ring of fire above the angel instead of a halo, and he carried an unsheathed sword. He held the sword above Reb Jehudah's head.

It was Samael, the Angel of Death.

Reb Jehudah did not notice this angel any more than he had noticed the others, for he was much too busy poring over the books of the law.

The Angel of Death shuddered. He knew that as long as the rabbi was engaged in his studies, his life could not be taken.

All this Moishe saw, peeping through the window, for he had come every day to watch over Rabbi Jehudah instead of attending heder or working on his father's farm. As if he were another angel, though a bit grubby, with a smudge on one cheek and his fingernails not quite clean.

When Moishe saw the eighth angel, he shook all over with fear. He recognized Samael. He had heard about that sword with its bitter drop of poison at the tip. "The supreme poison," his teacher had called it.

"Reb Jehudah," Moishe called, "beware!"

The rabbi, intent on his studies, never heard the boy. But the Angel of Death did. He turned his awful head toward the window and smiled.

It was not a pleasant smile.

And before Moishe could duck or run, the Angel of Death was by his side.

"I will have one from this village today," said the angel. "If it cannot be the rabbi, then it shall be you." And he held his sword above Moishe's head.

Seized by terror, the child gasped, and his mouth opened wide to receive the poison drop.

At that very moment, the seven angels in Reb Jehudah's house set up a terrible wail; and this, at last, broke the good rabbi's concentration. He stood, stretched, and looked out of the window to the garden that he loved, it being as beautiful to him as the Garden of Eden. He saw a boy at his window gasping for breath. Without a thought more, the rabbi ran outside and put his arms around the boy to try and stop the convulsions.

Head up, the rabbi prayed, "O Lord of All Creation, may this child not die."

The minute the rabbi's mouth opened, the poison drop from the sword fell into it, and he died.

The Angel of Death flew away, his errand accomplished. He would not be back in Ykaterinislav until early spring, for a pogrom. But the seven angels flew out of the open window, gathered up Reb Jehudah's soul, and carried it off to Heaven, where Metatron himself embraced the rabbi and called him blessed.

All this young Moishe saw, but he knew he could not tell anyone in Ykaterinislav. No one would believe him.

Instead he became a great storyteller, one of the greatest the world has ever known. His tales went around the earth, inspiring artists and musicians, settling children in their cots, and making the evenings when the tales were read aloud as sweet as nights in Paradise. "It was as if," one critic said of him, "his stories were carried on the wings of angels."

And perhaps they were.

I actually heard about the Jewish custom of "fooling the Angel of Death" from Ronnie Zusman, a Massachusetts woman whose grandmother's parents sold their own daughter this way to the neighbors. Of course they took her right back, but she then had the neighbors' last name, so the angel was—presumably—fooled.

I used my own grandmother's name in the poem, Manya (called Mina) Yolen. She had eleven children, three of whom were taken by the Angel on a single day by smallpox. The next-to-youngest of her eight living children was my father.

Manya's Story

Fearing the Angel of Death,
who already had three of their children,
Manya's parents sold her to the neighbors—
to fool the dark-winged one,
the black-eyed one,
the serpent of God.
It must have worked.
Manya grew to a mighty age,
had seven children,
twenty-seven grandchildren,
of whom my next-door neighbor is one.
This is no lie.
It is a story
embroidered by custom,
embellished by time.

My husband and I, along with his brother and wife, were visiting the lovely seventeenth-century town of Culross in Scotland. The place almost looks like a movie set, so perfectly preserved are the houses with their red pantile roofs. The narrow cobbled streets make driving difficult, but what a place to walk around!

We were in the "palace," which is really a merchant's house restored by the National Trust, and I was having a wonderful time in the terraced garden when a butterfly flew off to my left, just at the edge of my field of vision. All I glimpsed was something white and fluttery. As I was already deep into writing stories and poems for this book, and Culross is where Saint Mungo was born, I quite naturally started thinking about a story in which a seventeenth-century girl finds an angel in her terraced garden.

I scribbled down the few opening paragraphs (now greatly changed) on index cards before I forgot my ideas. Angel, garden, and Lady Merion were there from the start. But Clyve and kitchen maids were not. My brother-in-law, Dick Stemple, thought the angel should fly into the kitchen, and so it does. But I did not put in the angel food cake that Dick also thought should be there. This is my story, after all! The rest came slowly, two or three pages at a time, over a period of ten days.

I had to have help from my friend Bob Harris with the Latin. Like Lady Merion, I was not particularly attentive to my lessons way back in high school, especially the vocative case.

Lady Merion's Angel

Lady Merion was working in the garden when she saw the angel. She should have been at her half brother Clyve's second birthday party, but she was furious with him. He had gotten into her room again and this time he had ruined her embroidery. The angel was a welcome distraction.

It happened like this.

Lady Merion had just passed the wattle fencing, on which a hardy clematis still climbed, when something flew off, white and fluttery, to her left.

She turned, opened her mouth to scream, thought better of it, and coughed instead. Screaming was something a child would do. Like Clyve. At age fourteen, Lady Merion was now a young woman.

The something was hovering over one of the plawm trees. Lady Merion got a good look at it. It was definitely an angel; small, but not small enough to be a fairy. Its wings were white and feathered, rather than veined like a church window.

But why, Lady Merion wondered, *is an angel in the garden?* It was her own garden, and she was proud of it, nicely terraced with a fine view over the firth. But it was a work in progress, and nowhere near as perfect as the garden next door in the priory.

She chased the angel from the fruit trees, afraid it might try to land and in the process break off one of the precious branches. Then she shooed it with her apron past the terrace wall, where the brambles would soon flower, and into the kailyard.

"Pesky creature," Lady Merion cried. "Go and visit the priory, where you surely belong."

But the angel, small and plump and quite naked, settled over the rose arbor. It seemed to be waiting for her.

Lady Merion might be unnerved by the presence of an angel, but she was far from a stupid girl. The angel looked to be the same age as Clyve, whom she called the Town Crier, though not where her stepmother could hear. And if the angel was as stubborn as Clyve, getting a message out of it would be a miracle. But clearly it had one to deliver.

"Tell me," said Lady Merion. "Tell me now."

But the angel was silent.

23

"Oh, God's teeth!" Lady Merion said in disgust. It was not something she would ordinarily say out loud.

The angel fluttered about a foot higher, as if to give the oath plenty of room. Then it flew down in front of her.

"I have given you leave to speak," Lady Merion said. "So speak!"
But the angel remained silent.

Lady Merion's frustration with the creature was growing. Still she stared at it, as if by examining it carefully she could find in its very corporeal being some meaning. The angel's skin was as sweetly pink as a baby's, with the same round flesh that Clyve had. Its eyes were gooseberry green, not at all like Clyve's, which were like small round blue pebbles washed up on shore. There was an aura around the angel, a kind of apricot color that shimmered in the sun. Lady Merion wondered idly if the aura afforded any kind of protection from the rain. It rained a lot north of the firth.

The angel's wings beat quickly, like the wings of a bumblebee, and it took off through the open door into the kitchen.

Oh, my! Lady Merion thought, remembering the cake for Clyve's birthday celebration, and how goosey the scullery maid could be. She hurried after the angel.

By the time she got inside, the entire kitchen was in an uproar. Cook had a broom out and was trying to swat the angel, who darted about overhead, almost colliding with the hanging pans. The goosey scullery maid was having loud fits in the corner.

I wish she would faint already, Lady Merion thought, not at all charitably.

Three of the four kitchen girls were waving their aprons futilely, while the fourth had her apron up over her head.

"For pity's sake," Lady Merion said, this time aloud and loudly. "Stop your caterwauling" (this to the scullery maid). "And put down

that broom" (to Cook). "If you break something, my stepmother will have your head."

Cook stopped in midswing. The new lady of the manor came from somewhere north of Inverness, where her father, one of those Highlander chieftains, was known to behead felons with his own sword. Merion's threat was not to be taken lightly.

"And an angel is not a bat to tangle in your hair," Lady Merion said to the others. "Put your aprons down and get back to work. There is plenty enough to do for my brother's party. I shall deal with our . . . intruder." For it occurred to her now that the little angel had probably forgotten its message by this time, if it had ever had one in the first place. It was perched, rather disconsolately, atop the pantry cupboard, with its wings drooping and an unbecoming pout on its mouth.

Slowly the kitchen got back to order and Cook put the finishing touches on Clyve's cake, which was shaped—rather improbably—like a horse with sugared-frosting reins.

Lady Merion gently closed the door back out to the garden so the angel would not escape that way. Then, taking the broom that Cook had so hastily discarded, she slowly advanced on the cupboard, all the while making little assuring noises, as she might do to a frightened cat or lamb. When she got up to the cupboard, she carefully slid the stick end of the broom along the top edge till the tip was just under one of the angel's wings.

Tip-tap. She touched the wing lightly.

The little angel looked at the stick and, sensing no menace, giggled.

It was not what Lady Merion had expected, but the sound sent a delightful tickle up her back; behind her, three of the four maids began to laugh.

"Hop on," Lady Merion said to the angel. "Before you cause more of an outrage. You wouldn't want to meet my stepmother. Trust me."

26

She was surprised when the angel did as it was bidden, straddling the stick like a hobbyhorse and kicking out its little heels.

Holding the broomstick straight out, Lady Merion marched through the door and into the barrel-vaulted dining hall. The angel rode the stick with ease, burbling and bubbling.

They went through door after door till they came, at last, to Lady Merion's own chamber, with its painted ceiling and her mother's four-poster bed.

She set the broom on the bed, careful not to knock it against any of the posts or the oak canopy.

"There," she said to the angel. "Now climb down and let's hear what you have to say. It's quieter in here. Aids the memory."

The little angel looked at her and blew air into its cheeks, but it said nothing.

"God's teeth!" This time Lady Merion said it quite loudly.

The angel's mouth dropped open in shock.

"I am not sure which is worse," Lady Merion said to the angel. "An angel who giggles or one who acts like my great-aunt, the Dowager Lady Martin."

The angel cocked its head to one side.

"At least I've got your attention," Lady Merion said.

The angel continued to stare at her.

"So—do you have something to say?"

The angel was silent.

"Perhaps you do not understand English. Bother." Lady Merion had never been particularly attentive to her Latin tutor. She preferred gardening . . . In fact, the fruit trees had been her own idea. Her father—before he had remarried and gotten himself a son—had been quite proud of her gardening skills. At her request, he had secured grafts of a variety of fruit trees for her tenth birthday from a relative in Chagford, down in England. But nowadays he scarcely deigned to

27

walk along the crushed-rock pathways she had so carefully designed.

She went to her desk and took up her Latin grammar book, so long disused it was quite covered with dust. She blew the dust off, wrinkling her nose to keep from sneezing. *How does one address an angel in Latin?* She did not know the vocative. Or at least she did not remember how to use it.

"*Ave angelus?*" she said tentatively.

The angel did not respond.

"*Ave angeli?*"

Nothing.

"*Angelorum?*"

The silence continued.

"God's wounds!" It was a curse she had heard her father's latest visitor from Edinburgh say with much vehemence when his horse stepped on his new boot, and she had never dared use it in company. *But how much company is a silent angel?*

This oath so startled the angel that it rose straight up and hit the wooden canopy with its head. It cried out once and plummeted straight down onto the bed.

Without apology, Lady Merion put her hands on her hips. "Do not tell me you speak Hebrew. Latin is bad enough. But I could have just managed that."

The angel did not say a word, but it rubbed the top of its little head; and a single tear, translucent and pure as the water in a mountain stream, fell from its eye.

Without stopping to think why, Lady Merion sat down on the bed and gathered the little creature up in her arms. "There, there," she said. The angel felt warm and nicely squishy, like Clyve right after his bath. But the angel smelled much sweeter than ever Clyve did, a smell compounded of lavender and lily. She kissed the top of its head, where a slight red mark showed under the downy hair. "There, there."

The room was suddenly golden with light and crowded with angels, some dark as plawms, some light as peaches. Their fluttering wings made a humming.

"Give us our naughty child," said one angel, in perfectly good English with just the hint of an Oxford accent.

Lady Merion stared. "I most certainly will not. How do I know it's yours?"

"Don't be tiresome, child," another said in a plawmmy voice.

"I am not tiresome in the least," said Lady Merion. "Nor am I a child. I am fourteen, and fully old enough for marriage." Not that she wanted to get married and leave her garden to her father's new wife to ruin.

The angels conferred hastily, and then the darkest one descended the air as if going down steps till it was right by the bed though not exactly standing upon the floor. Finally it spoke to her directly.

"Give us the child and we will give you your heart's desire."

There was an odd smell coming from the angel, and it was not— Lady Merion was sure—either lavender or lily. She knew her flowers. This smell was more compost and rot.

"And what is my heart's desire?" Lady Merion asked.

"The . . . removal of your stepmother and half brother. The trees to quicken in your garden. Your father to turn his face once more to you." The angel said these things in measured tones, round and perfect. But somehow, said that way it all sounded . . . pitiful. And childish.

The angel in Lady Merion's arms looked up at her with a face as innocent as Clyve's. It smiled and it trembled a little, which she would not have noticed if she hadn't been holding it in her arms.

"I think not," she said. She had seen how harshly her stepmother had punished Clyve for making a mess of Merion's embroidery. "It hasn't been that naughty."

29

"But angels are supposed to be . . . perfect," the angel said. Its voice, Lady Merion noticed, had no modulation either up or down, but rather remained on one note, as if it were chanting.

"But it is just a wee thing," Lady Merion pointed out, and then had the grace to laugh—as that was just what Nurse had tried to say to Lady Merion herself when Clyve had so tangled her tapestry.

The angel smiled and was suddenly transformed into a glowing being. "That will be counted in the child's favor," the large dark angel said. "And yours." And with a fluttering of wings, the host of angels rose through the ceiling and were gone.

The little angel stood up on the bed, turned to her, and kissed her on the cheek. Merion felt as if she had been burned by a brand. And then the little angel was gone, too, after the others, its wings beating apace.

"Well . . . !" Lady Merion said at last. When she stood, a single small white feather fell from her lap and sailed lazily to the floor. She looked down at it for a moment, then stooped and picked it up thoughtfully. If she shaved the nib down and tied one of her best red ribbands around it, Clyve might love it for a birthday present. Until she could make something more suitable. Like a tapestry full of horses for his room.

And smiling, she went to find how much of the party she had actually missed.

After I graduated from college, I moved to New York City to work as an editor. One of the first people I met was Gustav Davidson, who ran the Poetry Society of America. Because I was an aspiring young poet, he and his wife took me under their wing. Davidson is the author of A Dictionary of Angels, *still the most important compendium of angel lore, and he gave me a signed copy.*

One day when I was thumbing through the book, I discovered Pistis Sophia, the angel who—according to Davidson—put the serpent in the garden of Eden. The following story, in its entirety, sprang into my mind. It has been reprinted many times, including in The World's Best Fantasy Short Shorts, *edited by Isaac Asimov, which was very gratifying.*

Angelica

The boy could not sleep. It was hot and he had been sick for so long. All night his head had throbbed. Finally he sat up and managed to get out of bed. He went down the stairs without stumbling.

Elated at his progress, he slipped from the house without waking either his mother or father. His goal was the riverbank. He had not been there in a month.

He had always considered the riverbank his own. No one else in the family ever went there. He liked to set his feet in the damp ground and make patterns. It was like a picture, and the artist in him appreciated the primitive beauty.

Heat lightning jetted across the sky. He sat down on a fallen log and picked at the bark as he would a scab. He could feel the log imprint itself on his backside through the thin cotton pajamas. He wished—not for the first time—that he could be allowed to sleep without his clothes.

31

The silence and heat enveloped him. He closed his eyes and dreamed of sleep, but his head still throbbed. He had never been out at night by himself before. A slight touch of fear was both pleasure and pain.

He thought about that fear, probing it like a loose tooth, now to feel the ache and now to feel the sweetness, when the faint came upon him and he tumbled slowly from the log. There was nothing but riverbank before him, nothing to slow his descent, and he rolled down the slight hill and into the river, not waking till the shock of the water hit him.

It was cold and unpleasantly muddy. He thrashed about. The sour water got in his mouth and made him gag.

Suddenly someone took his arm and pulled him up onto the bank, dragged him up the slight incline.

He opened his eyes and shook his head to get the lank, wet hair from his face. He was surprised to find that his rescuer was a girl, about his size, in a white cotton shift. She was not muddied at all from her efforts. His one thought before she heaved him over the top of the bank and helped him back onto the log was that she must be quite marvelously strong.

"Thank you," he said when he was seated again, and then did not know where to go from there.

"You are welcome." Her voice was low, her speech precise, almost old-fashioned in its carefulness. He realized that she was not a girl but a small woman.

"You fell in," she said.

"Yes."

She sat down beside him and looked into his eyes, smiling. He wondered how he could see her so well when the moon was behind her. She seemed to light up from within, like some kind of lamp. Her

outline was a golden glow and her blond hair fell in straight lengths to her shoulders.

"You may call me Angelica," she said.

"Is that your name?"

She laughed. "No. No, it is not. And how perceptive of you to guess."

"Is it an alias?" He knew about such things. His father was a customs official and told the family stories at the table about his work.

"It is the name I . . ." She hesitated for a moment and looked behind her. Then she turned and laughed again. "It is the name I travel under."

"Oh."

"You could not pronounce my real name," she said.

"Could I try?"

"Pistis Sophia!" said the woman, and she stood as she named herself. She seemed to shimmer and grow at her own words, but the boy thought that might be the fever in his head, though he hadn't a headache anymore.

"Pissta . . ." He could not stumble around the name. There seemed to be something blocking his tongue. "I guess I better call you Angelica for now," he said.

"For now," she agreed.

He smiled shyly at her. "My name is Addie," he said.

"I know."

"How do you know? Do I look like an Addie? It means—"

"'Noble hero,'" she finished for him.

"How do you know that?"

"I am very wise," she said. "And names are important to me. To all of us. Destiny is in names." She smiled, but her smile was not so pleasant any longer. She started to reach for his hand, but he drew back.

"You shouldn't boast," he said. "About being wise. It's not nice."

"I am not boasting." She found his hand and held it in hers. Her touch was cool and infinitely soothing. She reached over with the other hand and put first its palm, then its back to his forehead. She made a *tch* against her teeth and scowled. "Your guardian should be Flung Over. I shall have to speak to Uriel about this. Letting you out with such a fever."

"Nobody *let* me out," said the boy. "I let myself out. No one knows I am here—except you."

"Well, there is one who *should* know where you are. And he shall certainly hear from me about this." She stood up and was suddenly much taller than the boy. "Come. Back to the house with you. You should be in bed." She reached down the front of her white shift and brought up a silver bottle on a chain. "You must take a sip of this now. It will help you sleep."

"Will you come back with me?" the boy asked after taking a drink.

"Just a little way." She held his hand as they went.

He looked back once, to see his footprints in the rain-soft earth. They marched in an orderly line behind him. He could not see hers at all.

"Do you believe, little Addie?" Her voice seemed to come from a long way off, farther even than the hills.

"Believe in what?"

"In God. Do you believe that he directs all our movements?"

"I sing in the church choir," he said, hoping it was the proof she wanted.

"That will do for now," she said.

There was a fierceness in her voice that made him turn in the muddy furrow and look at her. She towered above him, all white and gold and glowing. The moon haloed her head, and behind her, close to her shoulders, he saw something like wings, feathery and waving. He was suddenly desperately afraid.

35

"What are you?" he whispered.

"What do you think I am?" she asked, and her face looked carved in stone, so white her skin and black her features.

"Are you . . . the Angel of Death?" he asked, and then looked down before she answered. He could not bear to watch her talk.

"For you, I am an angel of life," she said. "Did I not save you?"

"What kind of angel are you?" he whispered, falling to his knees before her.

She lifted him up and cradled him in her arms. She sang him a lullaby in a language he did not know. "I told you in the beginning who I am," she murmured to the sleeping boy. "I am Pistis Sophia, Angel of Wisdom and Faith. The one who put the serpent into the garden, little Adolf. But I was only following orders."

Her wings unfurled behind her. She pumped them once, twice, and then the great wind they commanded lifted her into the air. She flew without a sound to the Hitler house and left the boy sleeping, feverless, in his bed.

The story of the angelic figures seen by English soldiers during World War I has been attested to by the soldiers themselves. It was late August 1914, and the Germans were massing for a final push against the outnumbered British troops near the town of Mons. The British fully expected to be annihilated. A small detachment hastily erected a barricade, preparing to try and slow down the German advance so that some of their compatriots might escape. They prayed. And then—suddenly—four or five large shining beings seemed to interpose themselves between the British and their enemies. The German cavalry horses refused to move forward, and the German soldiers, dazed and disordered, unaccountably fled.

At least that is the story that has been reported.

I wrote this poem in the voice of a young English soldier—probably a lieutenant, as he has been to a university. He is writing to his mother the day after the incident at Mons, trying to explain it both to her and to himself. The poem seemed to write itself in a single day. I did four drafts—and then it was done.

The Angels of Mons

August 24, 1914

Mother:
I hope this letter finds you well.
I have gone from certain Hell
To Heaven in a single day.
There is simply no other way
To tell it. We were on the run,
Taking a pounding from the German gun-
Fire. We set up a hasty barricade

Under the brutal sun. No shade
To disguise this, our final stand.
We turned toward the enemy, manned
Our posts, said a soldier's prayer,
Knew we were going to die there,
There in the mud of a foreign land.

Mother:
I hope this letter finds you—well,
I hesitate. The rest is difficult to tell
Without sounding the complete and utter fool.
There is simply no rule
For this sort of thing. Nothing learned
In university; no special merit earned
Me this favour from Heaven. But where I
Stood, prepared to die, the certain sky
Opened with a bright and shining light.
And there—between two armies readied to fight—
Flew five luminous beings, arms upraised
As if a greater god than war were praised
There in the mud of a foreign land.

Mother:
I hope this letter finds you well.
There is more of this miracle to tell.
The German horses swerved, shied, fled.
We who had thought to die were not dead
But in the presence of something greater than Death:
Greater than guns, than life, than breath.
Angels, Mother, what else could they be?
And we, so sure of eternity,

Could scarce believe the evidence of our own eyes
As they floated down from the credible skies
Between us and the German foe.
This, dear Mother, is all I know.
Written from the mud of a foreign land.

                    Your loving son.

Early in our marriage, my husband and I spent almost a year camping in Europe and the Middle East. One of the places we traveled through was Thessaly, Greece, where it looked as if horses really were growing like wheat in the fields. It was there I first got the idea for the story of Aetos, the boy with wings. After I finished the story, though, I realized it was not the simple folk-like tale that I supposed. It was a parable of my life.

I had always been the odd one in any school I was in: the imaginative kid who loved to write. The kind of kid who was more at home in books than in life. But once I became a published author, whose books took flight, many of those acquaintances who had not paid me any attention began to correspond with me. All I had wanted in school was to be popular. I would have given away my wings if that had been a real option. Now, because of my books, I was.

The Boy Who Had Wings

In a village deep in Thessaly, where horses grow like wheat in the fields, a boy was born with wings. They were long, arching wings, softly feathered and golden-white in color. They moved with delicate grace. And they were like nothing ever seen before in the whole of the Thessalian plain.

The boy's parents named him Aetos, which means "eagle," because of his wondrous wings.

But Aetos's father, who was a herdsman, could not abide him. "Who has ever heard of a child with wings?" he asked, and made a sign with his hands to protect himself from evil spirits each time the child came near. "Surely the gods must be displeased with me to have sent me so strange a son. What good is he to me? He is something for wise men and fools to wonder about, but not a fit son for a keeper of horses."

41

And as Aetos grew from an infant to a boy, his father found one excuse after another to stay away from home, taking his herd of horses higher and higher into the surrounding hills.

At last he came home only when the driving rains made him seek shelter, or the drifting snows closed the mountain trails.

Now, Aetos's mother loved her son, but she, too, felt uneasy at the sight of his wings. Were they really a sign of the gods' disfavor? Or were they a blessing? It was hard to tell, but one dared not take chances. And if the villagers knew of this strange thing, they might do Aetos some hurt. So she made him a black goat-hair cape to cover his shoulders and forbade him ever to fly or to let people know of his wings.

And Aetos never disobeyed her.

But gradually Aetos became the forgotten one of the family. He played by himself in the corner of the house.

When shoved outside by his older brothers, he would wander alone down by the river. There, from behind a large olive tree, he would watch the women washing clothes in the water and the children playing on the shore.

Once in a while he would raise his eyes to the birds that raced the clouds across the skies. And sometimes his own wings would respond to the sight. They would try to stretch and arch. Then Aetos would pull his goat-hair cape more tightly around his thin shoulders and carefully study the ground until the wings were quiet once more.

It happened one day that the winter winds blew icily across the plain. Snow fell steadily in the mountains for a night and a day. But Aetos's father, high in the hills, did not come home. The snow had trapped him and his horses behind a wall of white.

The days grew colder. The winds came fiercely from the north. And still the herdsman could not bring his horses home.

In the village Aetos, his mother, and his two older brothers sat by the fire, shivering with the cold and wondering about the father.

Finally the oldest brother, Panos, arose. "I will try to find my father," he said. He took a leather pouch and filled it with olives and flat bread. Then he went out into the storm.

But scarcely a day later Panos returned. He had been able to go no farther than the foot of the mountain before the icy winds had driven him home.

So once more the herdsman's wife and his three sons sat by the fire. Finally the second brother, Nikos, arose. "Now it is my turn to seek our father," he said. He took the leather pouch and filled it with goat cheese and hung a goatskin full of wine from his belt. Then Nikos went out into the storm.

But scarcely two days later he returned. He had been able to go no farther than the first mountain pass before the icy winds and the wall of snow had driven him home.

So once more the herdsman's wife and his three sons sat by the fire. As the embers began to cool, Aetos arose. He pulled his goat-hair cape tightly around his shoulders. "It is left for me to seek our father," he said. "For if I had not been born with wings, he would have been safe at home even now."

And though he was still too young to brave the winter mountains all alone, neither his mother, nor Panos, nor Nikos told him no.

So, filling the leather pouch with a crust of dark bread and the goatskin with fresh milk, Aetos went out into the storm.

As he walked toward the mountain, the icy winds tore at his clothes. One chilling blast ripped the goatskin of milk from his shoulder and sent it spilling across the plain.

It does not matter, thought Aetos. *I will be lighter now.*

As Aetos reached the mountain's steep foot, a second chilling wind

tore the leather pouch from his belt and tossed it high up on the hills.

One thing less to carry, he thought. And he began to climb the snow-covered mountain.

Yet a third blast of the icy wind ripped his goat-hair cape from his shoulders, whipping it away like a giant black hawk.

Aetos uttered a sharp cry as the cold winter air found his shoulders and back, for suddenly, without his willing it, his wondrous wings arched against the wind, stretching high and pushing out beyond his shoulders. For a minute the wind seemed to grow gentle. It played with the feathers, stroking them, petting them. And then, before Aetos could think what to do, his golden-white wings had started to beat by themselves. High above the path they carried him, above the trees and above the mountain.

As he whirled, dipped, dived, and soared, Aetos felt happy and free for the first time in his life. He saw how small his house looked, how small the village looked, how small the mountain that imprisoned his father.

His father! In the joy of flying, Aetos had almost forgotten about his father, trapped behind the cold, white wall of snow. So he squinted his eyes in concentration and mastered the beating of his wings. Then carefully he glided down near the tops of the trees and began to search the steep sides and valleys for a sign of the herdsman and his herd.

At last he saw a few small, dark dots against the snow. Catching a current of air, he floated down to investigate. There, huddled between two mares shaggy in their winter coats, was his father, fainting with the cold.

Aetos swooped down and lifted his father into his arms. He marveled at how light his father felt, for the herdsman had gone many days with no food and only melted snow to drink. Then, with his wings beating against the cold air, the feathers beginning to stiffen

45

and grow heavy with ice, Aetos took off into the mountain air once again, his father cradled in his arms.

In less time than it takes to tell it, Aetos and his father had crossed up and over the mountain, sailed across the Thessalian plain, and landed in front of the herdsman's house.

Panos, Nikos, and their mother ran out and carried the herdsman inside, where they warmed him by the fire. But it was some time before they paid any heed to the chilled and drooping boy who shivered by the door. It was even longer before they noticed his frozen wings. But finally they signaled him to stand by the fire and filled him with warm broth and even warmer thanks.

The herdsman recovered quickly, for he was a hardy man. But Aetos lay in bed, shivering first cold and then hot, for many days.

When he was finally well, his wings, which had become frostbitten by the icy winds, lost all their feathers one by one. At last the wings themselves dropped off. All that was left were two large scars on his shoulders where the wings had been.

At first Aetos was sad, remembering the wild, happy freedom of his ride in the sky. But afterward, when both his mother and father hugged, kissed, petted, and praised him, and he was allowed to join the other boys at their games, he all but forgot about his lost wings. For they had brought him no happiness except in that one brief moment.

As the years passed and Aetos grew into a man, he was loved and respected by all. He lived as other men in the village did and became a herder of horses. His wings and his one great flight into freedom faded into a childhood memory. Except for the scars on his shoulders, he would have counted them as a dream. But now, no longer burdened by the wings, his soul could fly.

Yet, generations later, the people of the village were praying to a guardian angel of the horse herders, an angel they called Saint Aetos.

You see, the people never knew how unhappy the boy had been before he lost his wings, and only thought of how glorious it must be to fly. And boys and girls prayed each night to grow great, arched, golden-white wings that would carry them up over the mountains. Or they prayed that their own children might be born with such wings to bring them safely home across the plain.

But from that day to this, no one else has ever been so blessed.

Saint Augustine wrote, "Every visible thing in the world is put under the charge of an angel." What is more visible than the things we leave undone?

This simple poem took about five months to write. I thought a lot about the chores I used to leave undone as a child. (The worst was walking Mandy, our big black Labrador, who liked to chase squirrels. And mailmen.) And I thought about the chores my own children hated doing. I think we all hated the dishwashing the worst. Or emptying the cat's litter box. But I couldn't fit that in.

Child's Prayer

Angel of Things Undone—
Late homework, forgotten chores,
The dog not walked,
Soaking dishes,
Dirty socks on the bedroom floor,
Teeth not brushed, tub not scrubbed—
Forgive me.
Do not tell the Angel of Bad Dreams.

Brother Kenan's Bell

Brother Kenan woke in the night. He had had the most wondrous dream. An angel with a great smile of joy had come to him and said,

Take you a bell into the wilderness, a bell without clapper or tongue.
And when that bell shall ring by itself—there build a house of God.

When morning prayers were over, Brother Kenan hurried along the stone hall to the abbot's cell and told him of the dream.

"It *is* a strange dream," the abbot said, "for what is a bell without clapper or tongue?"

"A piece of metal?" asked Kenan.

"Just so," said the abbot with a smile. "A piece of metal. And do you think that I would send any of my monks into the wilderness with just a piece of metal to guide him? I am supposed to be a father to you all. What kind of a father would I be to let you go because of a single strange dream?"

Brother Kenan went into the monastery garden, where he was to work that day. There he saw Brother David and Brother John and told them about his dream.

Brother David, whose clever hands were never still, said, "Perhaps it was something you ate. Dreams often proceed from the stomach."

So Brother Kenan said no more.

But that night he dreamed again. This time the angel was not smiling, and said,

Take you a bell into the wilderness, a bell without clapper or tongue. And when that bell rings by itself—there build a house of God with Brother David and Brother John.

Brother Kenan did not even wait for the morning prayers to be rung. He put on his sandals and hurried off to the abbot's cell, where he roused the good father with a shake. The abbot was annoyed to be awakened before the bells, but he did not show it with his words or eyes. Only his mouth was angry and drawn into a hard line.

"It is certainly another strange dream," admitted the abbot. "But I myself have had many such dreams. Perhaps you are working too hard."

"But the angel knew Brother David's name," protested Kenan. "And he knew Brother John's name, too."

"Then he read your heart," said the abbot. "Surely an angel could do that." Then he turned over on his side and said, "Go back to bed, Brother Kenan."

After prayers Brother Kenan went to work in the monastery kitchen with Brother David and Brother John. He told them of his second dream.

51

Brother John, who could heal any ache with his herbs, said, "I have a simple that will help you sleep. And in *that* sleep you will not dream."

So Brother Kenan said no more.

But that night he dreamed again. This time the angel came and took him by the shoulder and shook him hard and said,

Take you a bell into the wilderness, a bell without clapper or tongue. And when that bell rings by itself—there build a house of God with Brother David and Brother John. AND DO IT SOON!

Brother Kenan did not even stop to put on his sandals. He hurried down the dark corridor to the abbot's cell. He burst in and was surprised to see the abbot sitting up in his bed. By his side were David and John.

"I have had yet another dream," began Kenan.

"Come," said the abbot with a great smile, and opened his arms. "So have we all. In the morning we must search for a piece of iron for your quest."

In the morning, after prayers, the three monks and the abbot looked all around the monastery for metal for the bell. But except for small nails and smaller needles, the pots and pans to cook the monastery meals, some rakes and hoes in the garden, and a knocker on the door, no metal could be found.

The abbot gave a large sigh. "I suppose I must give you our only bell," he said at last. "Come up with me to the bell tower."

So the four climbed to the top of the tower, high up where only Brother Angelus, the bell master, went. And there, lying under the chapel's bell, was an iron bar.

"I have never seen it before," said Brother Angelus with awe. "It is a miracle."

The abbot merely nodded and sighed again, this time in thanks.

Such miracles, he knew, often occurred when one was as old and as forgetful as the bell master. Still, when the four had descended the stairs, the abbot blessed the bar and gave it to Kenan.

"Go you must," he said, "so go with God."

The three monks left the monastery and took the road going north. Only to the north was the land empty of towns.

Brother Kenan was in the lead, carrying the iron bar like a banner before them.

Brother David was next, his pack filled with bread and cheese and string with which to practice knots, for his fingers always had to be busy with something.

Brother John was last, his basket filled with herbs and simples in case of any accidents or ills.

The three monks traveled for nearly three weeks. Their food ran out, and John found berries and mushrooms and roots. Their wine gave out, and David found a fresh flowing spring. Their spirits ran low, and Kenan cheered them on with a psalm. And always the silent iron bar went before.

One day, though, Brother David grew weary. He thought to himself, *Perhaps it was not a holy dream after all. I swear that that bell will never ring on its own. I must make the miracle happen.* So that night his clever fingers fashioned a sling out of the strings. And in the morning, as the monks marched along, he walked behind and aimed several small stones at the iron bar. But the stones went left or the stones went right. Each shot missed, and Brother Kenan marched on with the bell as silent as ever.

The next day Brother John grew weary. He thought to himself, *All dreams do not come from God. That bell will never ring by itself. Sometimes one must help a miracle along.* So he waited until he found a bush with hard, inedible berries growing along the path. He grabbed up a handful and threw the lot of them at Kenan's back. But the berries went left or the berries went right. Not one of them struck the bar. And Brother Kenan marched on with the bell as silent as ever.

The next day the monks came upon a broad meadow that stretched down to the banks of a tumbling stream.

This would be a lovely place to build a house of God, thought Kenan with a sigh, for he, too, was weary. But putting such a thought behind him as unworthy of his dream, he shouldered the iron bar and walked on.

Just then, a small brown bird flew across the meadow, fleeing from a hawk. The little bird ducked and dived to escape its pursuer, and in its flight it flew straight toward the three monks. At the last minute, noticing them, it turned sharply and rammed into the iron bar. It broke its wing and fell.

As the hawk veered off into the woods, the iron bar sang out from the collision, with a single clear and brilliant tone.

"The bell!" cried David and John as one.

"The bird!" cried Brother Kenan. He jammed the iron bar into the soft sod of the meadow and took up the wounded bird. And when he picked the bird up, the iron bar—standing straight and true in the meadow grass—rang out again and again and again. Each note was like a peal of hosannas to the Lord.

So the monks built their house of God in the meadow by the river. Brother David's wonderful hands and Brother John's wonderful simples cured the wounded bird. And with patient care, Brother Kenan melted down the iron bar and cast a perfect bell.

Ever after, the little brown bird sang outside Brother Kenan's window to call the many monks who worked in the abbey to their prayers. And its voice was as clear and as loud and as pure as the monks' own iron bell.

I first thought of this poem as a picture book. (I still do.) But I never found an editor who agreed with me.

I wanted my son Adam, who is a composer and musician, to set it to music. (He never did.) But every time I read it, I see pictures and hear a blues guitar playing mournfully in the background.

Angel City Blues

Streets of gold,
Streets of cloud,
Sing my blues
Right out loud:

I am here,
My dog is not.
Angel City Blues what I got.

Streets of silver,
Streets of sun.
Could play mouth harp—
Ain't no fun.

I am here,
My dog is not.
Angel City Blues what I got.

Streets of moon,
Streets of sky,

Wings unfurled,
Watch me fly.

High and low,
Not a lot.
Angel City Blues what I got.

Kick a stone,
Skip a star,
Trade you places
Where you are.

Ain't no dog
In this spot.
Angel City Blues what I got.

But—hear that sound
Low and long?
Train is coming,
Freight car song.
Hear that sound
Long and loud?
Bays clear through
Streets of cloud.
Hear that sound
Loud and wild?
Angel dog coming
After angel child.

Streets of silver,
Streets of gold.

Got the dog
I can hold.

Here I am.
Dog is, too.
Ain't no longer Angel City blue.

I am not only a writer, I am a professional storyteller as well. That means I get up in front of an audience and tell (act out) stories. Some of the tales are my own, but most come from folklore.

The following story I found some time ago in a book of African-American folktales, where it was only a couple of paragraphs long. As I have told the story over the years, it has grown and changed, but it is still basically the story out of that tradition, with Yolen curlicues.

The Word the Devil Made Up

Did you know there is a word the Devil made up? Well, there is. And it happened this way.

The Devil was sitting down in Hell and he was not happy. Work had been going badly. He simply did not have enough help. Now, if he were patient, he could have waited till the end of the week, when the new recruits were coming from Miami. But the Devil never has had any patience.

He thought, *I can go up to Heaven and grab me some angels. There are lots of them there.*

So he stood up on those cloven feet of his. He wrapped his tail around him three times and knotted it with a sailor's knot. (The Devil loves sailors.) Then he pumped his giant wings three times and flew up into the air.

He flew and he flew, and as he was passing Earth, he saw an old farmer hoeing his corn. The farmer had a shotgun by his side because his henhouse had been troubled of late by chicken hawks. And when he saw a giant winged creature fly by him, the farmer dropped the hoe and picked up the gun.

Whammity-blam. Whammity-blam. He fired off two blasts, but of course he missed. You can't hit the Devil with a shotgun.

Now, the Devil never even noticed, but he kept on flying right up to the gates of Heaven, which stood wide open. He walked in. There in front of him was a host of angels playing on their lyres.

The Devil scooped them up with his right hand.

And then he realized that he hadn't brought along a tote bag.

So he put those angels under his left arm. Right in the pit. The Devil knows a lot about pits.

But he looked around again because he wanted more angels. The Devil is *always* greedy.

And there he saw another host of angels, and they were playing on harps.

He scooped them up with his left hand and put them under his right arm. In the pit.

But then he looked around once again. Greedy Devil. And there he saw a host of angels playing kazoos.

"No one will miss them!" the Devil said. So he scooped them up. Now, he had no room under his right arm and no room under his left, so he jammed these angels into his mouth, and—careful not to grin (the Devil loves grinning)—he pumped his mighty wings and took off for home.

Now, as he passed Earth, that same farmer was hoeing his corn. Time passes differently for the Devil than for humans. And when the farmer saw something flying overhead, he grabbed up his shotgun and was set to fire it off again when he realized that chicken hawks don't have forty-foot wing spreads. And they are not bright red. And right off he guessed who it was. So he tipped his straw hat and said, "Howdy, Devil. Been out a-flying?" Just to make polite conversation.

And the Devil—who is always polite—answered him back.

"Yes," said the Devil. No more than that.

And all the angels jammed into the Devil's mouth flew out and up to Heaven.

Well, the Devil reached out to grab them with his right hand, and all the angels under his right arm flew out. So he reached out to catch *them* with his left hand, and all the angels under his left arm flew out.

They headed right back to Heaven and slammed the gates shut. And the gates have been shut tight ever since.

This made the Devil so mad he flew back down to Hell without even bidding that farmer farewell. And there the Devil sat on his bone throne in a grump. Well, he moaned and he groaned and he wrassled with his anger for a week. By that time the new recruits had come from Miami, so that was all right.

But in that time the Devil came up with a new word, one he could use instead of *yes* or *no* without ever opening his mouth. That word was *unh-hunh. UNH-HUNH!*

Can you say it? Can you?

Unh-hunh!

Oh, you little devil!

Sometimes a story comes piecemeal and sometimes it comes in one piece. This story is a bit of both. I thought of the opening paragraph as I was flying to Scotland for a working vacation. (That is, it's a vacation just to be in Scotland, but I had work to do nonetheless.)

By the time I had gotten hold of a typewriter, I knew there were going to be three children in the story to help the fallen angel. And after mentioning the story to my editor on a transatlantic phone call, I knew what their reward was going to be. But I didn't know anything else.

Writing the story took me more than a week, made longer by the fact that my brother-in-law and his wife had come for a visit and we were touring them around the places in Scotland that we love. (I mean the first draft of the story took a bit over a week. Rewriting it took another week. The final draft was completed a month later. Sometimes stories have to sit around, settling down in their bones. The same goes for the writer.)

About those three children: I have three myself, but mine are two boys and a girl. I have a new granddaughter named Maddy and I borrowed her name for the story. I also borrowed my middle son's Grateful Dead T-shirt, for as I was writing this story the news came that the lead guitarist for the Dead, Jerry Garcia, had just died. And the things the mother in the story says when she is working on her novel—well, I used to say them when my own children interrupted me at work. So I borrowed from myself as well.

Fallen Angel

Down and down and down he fell, his wings wrapped around him for warmth. They were now useless for flying, the feathers having been severely burned in the awful flames.

Angels are ordinarily immune to the terrible cold of space, but featherless, he was freezing. The slight warmth lent him by the wings'

65

structure was not enough. His teeth chattered and he shivered uncontrollably as he fell.

His passage was a long flash of light.

"I saw the most amazing falling star last night," Courtney said. "It was the brightest ever."

"I saw it, too," Maddy said. "Do you think it was a USO?"

"U-F-O, dummy!" Judson thought his younger sister could be positively stupid sometimes.

"Or an alien?" Maddy continued, unconcerned with Judson or his frequent judgments.

"Dad says there's no such thing," Judson said—always his final argument.

"It was so bright. It looked like it fell right into Miller's Pond."

"It did!" Maddy confirmed. "Right in. An alien!"

"No such thing." Judson couldn't have been more definite. He wanted to be a scientist when he grew up. But he went along to the pond with the others, in the cause of scientific accuracy, of course.

The angel lay curled in the mud by the pond, his white gown still pristine but his glorious hair for once in tangles. His wings looked like leafless fronds. There was a smudge of mud along one cheekbone. He breathed heavily through his aquiline nose.

The children ringed him around. Maddy put her thumb in her mouth, something she did in moments of great stress or concentration.

"Do you think it's a woman?" Judson asked. "Or a man?" It was really difficult to tell. The broad shoulders and large hands seemed to argue for a man; the gown and long red hair, the perfect beauty, for a woman.

"An alien," said Maddy, the thumb popping out of her mouth like a cork from a bottle.

66

"An angel," said Courtney.

And they all knew the moment she said it that she was right.

"But what about the . . . um . . . ?" Judson asked, running a hand through his hair nervously. He wondered if scientists were allowed to discover angels. "Those don't exactly look like wings, you know."

"Angels have wings," Maddy said. But she said it hesitantly, as if she were suddenly uncertain about the call. The thumb went back in her mouth.

"Those *are* the wings," Courtney said, pointing to the frondlike structures fanning out from the angel's back. "Only broken and burned."

"Re-entry!" Judson said, happy to be on scientific ground again. "Like rockets coming back from space. I don't suppose angels carry heat shields."

"Like a falling star," Courtney said.

Maddy had no idea what the older two were talking about, but she had been the only one watching the angel while they chattered. "'ook!" she cried, then took the thumb from her mouth. "Look!"

They looked. The angel had opened one eye. It was sky blue and perfect.

What the angel saw with that one eye was this: a twelve-year-old girl with hair the color of a mouse's back, who had the day before sneaked a drag on a cigarette and hated it, but lied to her friends saying she liked it a lot, and worried more about that lie than the one puff; a ten-year-old boy, his hair cut in a rattail, who had called his older sister a forbidden name the night before to his friends and was feeling awful about it because actually he secretly admired her; a girl age seven, in braids, who had taken her sister's favorite comb but had only the slightest guilt associated with it since she was planning to give it back, so the angel could not tell the size or shape of the comb. All this the angel saw in a blink of his perfect eye.

"*A*l*l*e*l*u*j*a*h*," sang the angel. And then he said, "*O*u*c*h*," because his wings hurt. It was a strange sound for a strange sensation. Angel wings *never* hurt.

"The angel spoke!" Maddy cried, but since they had all heard it, Judson elbowed her roughly to make her shut up.

The angel made a sound like *tch* with his perfect mouth, and Judson felt immediate shame, a shame so deep and profound that his face turned crimson from the neck up and he had to look away or sob.

"Sorry, Maddy," he whispered.

"*T*e* *a*b*s*o*l*v*o*!" said the angel. When it was clear none of the children understood this, he closed his perfect eye and heard inside the language that they had been speaking. He opened the eye again. "*I*t*'*s* *o*k*a*y*," he sang, but the words seemed clumsy in his mouth, faithless. They lacked the beauty of Latin, the power of Hebrew, the familiarity of Aramaic or Greek. But they were all these children knew, so they would have to do.

"Are you—like—an angel?" Courtney asked at last.

The angel looked puzzled. "*L*i*k*e*?" Then, receiving no response from the children, he added in speech rather than song, "Very like."

"He means he is," said Maddy, her thumb nowhere near her mouth now.

"He means"—Judson was adamant—"sort of."

"How can he be *sort of* when he is *very* like?" Courtney said.

"*S*T*O*P*!" the angel sang out. Children of this era, it seemed, were enough to try even an angel's patience.

The children were stunned into silence.

"I am an angel."

"Oh!" They said it all together, as if they couldn't quite believe it and yet had to, a kind of resignation tinged with awe. "Oh!"

The angel was pleased with their response and sat up. Or at least he tried to sit up. But he was awkward, which made him feel so unlike himself that, for a moment, he actually hesitated.

Courtney leaned over and grabbed his left arm, Judson his right. Maddy touched his white gown and gave the hem a little tug. Together they managed to help the angel sit. His wings, featherless and brittle, drooped behind.

"You hardly weigh anything," Courtney remarked.

"I am insubstantial," the angel replied.

"Not exactly," Judson said. "You do weigh *something*. Just not a lot. Maybe gravity is different here than . . ." For a moment he was stumped. "Than in . . . wherever."

"Heaven," Maddy said.

The angel smiled. His teeth were perfect.

"We don't believe in Heaven," Judson reminded her.

"I do," Maddy said.

"*You* are seven," said Judson.

"So?"

"So what do you know?"

"Maybe"—Courtney interrupted them—"maybe Heaven is a real place, so believing doesn't count, and—"

"*E*N*O*U*G*H*!"

They shut up and stared at the angel—a bit resentfully. Their parents had always encouraged the spirit of inquiry in them. The dinner table was a daily free-for-all.

The angel was beginning to suspect that Earth had changed in the millennia since he had last visited. In those days belief had been a constant, and children had not argued or spoken out of turn, and he had had wings that worked and did not hurt.

Suddenly the angel hated all change. Which was an odd thing in itself, as it was the very changeless nature of Heaven that was the cause of his present misfortune. Hadn't he tried to change things just

69

a bit? Which had provoked the flames, which had led to his wings' being seared, and thence to his falling down and down and down. The memory of the fall was suddenly quite vivid, and the angel felt faint.

"I want," the angel said aloud and in perfect English, "to go home." He cried a perfect tear.

Maddy's thumb went back into her mouth, and Courtney patted the angel's shoulder. "Everything will be all right. You'll go back. Of course you will."

"Not with those wings," said Judson.

And they all knew—even the angel—that he was right.

They talked about it till shadows began to form around the pond. The angel occasionally sniffled, more like a child than a grown-up. They talked about feathers, about birds, about outer space. The angel told them all about Heaven, too, which they did not entirely credit.

"It sounds incredibly boring," said Judson, who couldn't stand to be bored, not for a minute. "All that marching about in formation. And singing."

"And so clean." Maddy had smudges on her nose and around her mouth, mostly from popping her thumb in and out. She was not normally a clean child by any means.

"But it's home," Courtney explained with a great deal more patience than she usually showed. "And that's why he misses it."

"So he should," agreed Maddy.

But Judson did not agree. He rolled his eyes up till only the whites showed. "If I had to sing all day . . . *A*l*l*e*l*u*j*a*h*!" He gave a remarkably good imitation of the angel, even though he was not on pitch. "And if I had to be grateful and gracious or any other *g* word to someone mighty, I would have taken a jump, too."

"Good," said Maddy.

"Good what?" Judson was puzzled.

"Another *g* word the angel has to be."

The angel stood. "The dark is coming and I am afraid, not being used to darkness."

Courtney stood, too, and put out her hand. "Then come home with us. Mommy and Daddy won't mind."

Which they didn't, because neither of them could see the angel. Not his perfect eyes or perfect teeth or perfect smile. Not his perfect white gown or perfect red hair. Or his bedraggled, seared, and drooping wings.

"I don't understand," said Judson as they led the angel from the living room, where they had tried unsuccessfully to introduce the angel to Mommy and Daddy.

Mommy had looked up and said, "Can *who* stay in the guest room, dear?"

And Daddy had said, "Invisible playmate, darling."

Mommy had answered, "Aren't they a little old for that?"

And Daddy had responded, "Encourage imagination, sweetheart. You of all people . . ."

So they had put the angel in the guest room anyway, with its double bed and bear-claw quilt. There was an electrified candle sconce for a bedside light.

"You can put your gown in the closet," Courtney said. "There are hangers."

"Or fold it up and put it in the dresser," added Maddy. "Do you know how to do that? I could teach you." She had learned how in Montessori school.

"Or just throw it down by the bed," Judson said. "I do. My shirt, that is. I don't wear a gown. Boys don't, you know."

71

"Why would I take my gown off?" the angel asked. *"How* would I take it off?"

"Because it's dirty," said Courtney. "You've been in it all day, in the mud and everything."

"Angels don't get dirty," Maddy reminded her, "'member?"

"That's in Heaven," said Judson. "Not on earth."

About that time they realized that the angel could not have taken off the gown even if he wanted to.

"There are no wing holes!" Courtney said. "Or at least not any big enough to pull wings through. How did you get it on in the first place?"

"There was no first place," said the angel. "I have always worn this gown." He said it as if that were explanation enough. And indeed it was all the explanation they were ever to get.

They said good night to him then. And since angels don't have to eat, they went down to their own supper. It was a children-only supper because Mommy and Daddy were having a dinner party for grown-ups later on, so the children could discuss the angel over the meal the entire time.

It was Judson who first mentioned making new wings. It was Courtney who remembered the swatches of material Aunt Isabelle—who did interior decorating—had sent them. But it was Maddy who got up from the meal silently and went to her room without explanation, returning with a large, battered box kite.

"That's it!" Judson said.

"Clever girl," added Courtney.

Maddy was much too full of herself to put her thumb back into her mouth. The only thing she put there was her dessert. And Courtney's as well, for Courtney was back on a diet.

"We'll have to get extra dowels, though," Judson said. "There aren't nearly enough."

72

"What's a dowel?" asked Maddy.

So he showed her. "These sticks."

"Do you think we've got enough material?" asked Courtney.

"Sheets?" asked Maddy.

"If we have to," Courtney said. "Though they aren't as tough as the stuff on those swatches, since that's drapery material. Has to be tough to stand up to outer space."

"To go where no angel has gone before," Judson intoned.

That started them giggling as they got up from the meal. Then— to forestall their mother asking questions—they cleared the table without being reminded.

"Invisible friend or not," Mommy remarked later to Daddy, "they *are* growing up. Imagine, clearing the supper dishes without my saying a word."

"Encourage responsibility, sweetheart," he answered, and went out to greet their arriving guests.

"Growing up," mused Mommy to herself, "or else up to something." But because the guests had all come at once, she didn't get a moment to check, and by the time her dinner party was in full swing she had forgotten all about it.

The children worked quietly in Courtney's room until nearly eleven. They got only one angel-sized wing made, using the old dowels from the battered kite and binding them with a combination of glue, tape, rubber bands, and an old lanyard Judson had made in Boy Scouts the one year he had gone to den meetings.

Courtney had used up half the thread in her sewing basket making vanes of the material—a veritable patchwork of curtain, sofa, and rug swatches that she attached to the dowels with a crochet stitch.

"Will it hold?" Maddy asked, coming over to look.

In answer, Courtney tugged on the material. The dowels bent

alarmingly but did not break, and the material—to everyone's relief—stayed firmly attached.

"But the angel needs two wings," said Maddy, moving back to the door, where she was acting as lookout.

Judson's face was grim. "And we are about out of everything."

"We'll think about that tomorrow," Courtney said.

Just then Maddy cried out, "Oh!", by which they knew the guests were going home.

"Tomorrow, then," Judson said before he sneaked down the hall.

"Tomorrow," Maddy echoed, going through the door into her own room.

Courtney nodded and pushed the wing into her closet. She was so tired from the work of the evening and the excitement of the day, she fell asleep still in her clothes and dreamed she was an angel. An angel with wings of flame.

In the morning Maddy came into Courtney's room leading the angel by the hand. His gown was as pristine white as it had been the day before, his red hair no longer in tangles. But he did not look quite as perfect as before. In fact he looked . . .

"Insubstantial!" said Courtney. She meant she could see through him, as if he were a bad photograph taken with too much light.

"You're fading," remarked Judson, coming into the room. "And you," he added accusingly to Courtney, "slept in your clothes. Mommy's going to be furious."

"But the angel slept in his," said Maddy.

"Mommy is not the angel's mother," Judson told her.

"I have no mother," the angel said. "Only a *f*a*t*h*e*r*."

"Poor angel," said Maddy, patting his hand. "You can share ours."

Courtney sat up on her bed, her legs tucked up under her. "We

75

made one wing for you," she said. "But we are going to have to figure out how to make another."

"We are out of . . . stuff," Judson explained.

"Towels," said Maddy.

"Dowels, stupid," said Judson. "With a *d*."

"I meant that," said Maddy.

"Sure you did," muttered Judson, but suddenly remembering his deep shame of the day before, he kept one eye on the angel.

The angel did not seem to notice, but he nodded his increasingly insubstantial head. The red curls bobbed with the effort.

"The angel didn't sleep well," Maddy said.

"Your mother turned out the light."

"She does that," Judson said, happy to be back on safer ground. And then in a remarkable imitation of his mother's voice, he added, "'Because once you're asleep, it doesn't matter.'" He grinned. "The light, I mean."

"The light," the angel said in a voice as hard as adamantine, "always matters."

Judson gulped aloud.

"But," the angel was quick to add, "it is not that I did not sleep *well*, dear children. I did not sleep at all."

"Poor angel," said Maddy.

The angel shook his head. "But I *never* sleep. Angels don't. Still, I was afraid of the dark all the night long. Though as nights go, I don't suppose it was especially long."

"Not in June," said Judson. "In June the nights are short."

"When you are scared," Courtney added, "fear makes things *seem* longer."

"And when you are happy," Maddy said, "things seem shorter."

Now the angel really looked perplexed. "I should think it would be the other way around."

"Long or short, we have got to make you another wing," Courtney said. "That means more dowels. And more material."

"But how?" asked the angel.

"We don't know yet," Courtney admitted. "But it doesn't mean we won't know soon. It's just going to take time."

The angel sat down on Courtney's bed, carefully folding his drooping wings behind him. They could see the double-wedding-ring quilt through him.

"I don't think we have all that much time," said Maddy. She popped her thumb determinedly into her mouth and looked very stressed indeed.

But though they sat for an hour discussing the wing, the children could come up with no real solution. They did, however, agree on three things: that it was useless to ask their parents, that it was dangerous to ask their parents, and that it was crazy to ask their parents.

So they did.

The angel did not understand this logic. But then he had never had children. Angels don't.

"We have found an angel, Mommy," Courtney said.

Hunched over her keyboard—the novel was *not* going well—Mommy looked up crossly.

"He sleeps in his clothes," Maddy said.

Judson rolled his eyes up until only the whites showed.

Mommy sighed. "And what does this angel need?"

"Wings," Judson said under his breath.

"Don't mumble, Juddie. You know I have a slightly deaf ear."

The children all thought Mommy was slightly deaf only when it suited her.

"It needs wings!" said Judson, almost shouting.

77

"If it needs wings, then it can't be an angel," Mommy said sensibly. "Angels already have wings."

"I told you," Judson whispered to his sisters, "that this was going to be useless."

"Now I am working. Remember, don't bother me unless you are"—and Mommy laughed gaily—"bleeding from an important orifice." She thought she was being clever.

The children had heard it before.

They went away.

"Daddy is at the university today, so there's no help there," said Courtney. "If only he were a regular father, he'd have a workshop in the garage instead of a lab off in town."

"With dowels," Judson said.

"What's a dowel?" Maddy asked automatically, and then, remembering that she already knew, stuck her thumb unhesitatingly in her mouth.

They went out into the garden and stripped several branches from a birch tree, but these were too bendy. Then they tried a track from Judson's model railroad set, but it didn't bend at all. They found an old telephone cord in the tool drawer, and that was impossible. Strips of cardboard didn't work either. Or knitting needles or crochet hooks or pipe cleaners.

"It's no good," Courtney said at last, almost in tears.

The angel sat silently on her bed. He was practically an outline, and his facial features kept fading in and out, in and out.

"Like the Cheshire Cat," said Judson, to no one in particular.

"I am cold," said the angel.

Maddy went immediately into Courtney's closet for something to throw over the angel's shoulders. She emerged without any clothing, but clutching a hanger. "What about this?" she asked.

"Hangers!" Judson and Courtney called out together.

"Brilliant," Courtney added.

"Genius!" said Judson. It was his highest compliment. "Absolute genius."

"There are lots more of them on the floor," Maddy said.

"I think they breed there," said Courtney.

Judson giggled.

While the angel watched, somewhat bemusedly, the children each gathered an armful of hangers. Slowly they twisted them out of hanger shape and fashioned a second wing. They taped the ends together, then tied them with the old telephone cord for good measure, so that the wing armature had a lovely shape and lumpy parts.

Then Courtney cut up a pair of her old blue jeans, ones that were much too small. "The heck with dieting," she said. "I'm never going to fit in these again." She checked to see if the angel had noticed the minor swear before cutting up her mother's Grateful Dead T-shirt, which Courtney had borrowed permanently several months before. Jeans and T-shirt went into the making of the wing vanes.

The end result was much more elegant than the first wing, and much more solid.

"Maybe we should do them both this way," Courtney said.

"No time!" Maddy pointed to the angel, whose outline was now wavering. Then she popped the pointing finger into her mouth.

They tied the new wings tightly to the angel's broken pair with ribbons from the Christmas box. The angel was quite a sight. But once they went outdoors and he unfolded the new wings, the patches of color caught the sun and he looked quite beautiful.

"Lovely," the angel said. Then he sang out, "*B*e*l*l*i*s*s*i*m*a*!*" He began to take on substance again.

"What's *bellissima?*" asked Maddy.

"I think it's *lovely* in Latin," said Courtney.

79

Maddy smiled. "Are you going to go home now?" she asked the angel.

"Up . . . there?" Judson added, waving an uncertain hand toward the sky.

"Heaven," Courtney whispered.

"If they will have me back," the angel said. "If *H*e* will let me in."

"How could He not?" said Maddy. "He's your daddy."

The angel smiled. It was a perfect smile. "Give me your hands, children."

They held out their hands to him and he enclosed them in his perfect palms.

"I will give you a reward for your unselfish help," he said. "Angels can do that, you know."

"We didn't do it for a reward," said Courtney, ending with a little squeal as Judson stepped solidly on her foot.

"Of course you didn't," said the angel. "That is what *unselfish* means."

"Could I have a new Barbie?" Maddy asked.

Judson interrupted. "I'd like a Pentium. And Windows 95. And—"

"World peace," Courtney said, closing her eyes. "That's what we all want. World peace."

"Not within my powers," said the angel. "But I can give you each contentment."

"What's contentment?" asked Maddy.

"Happiness," Courtney explained.

Clearly all three were disappointed.

"We are already happy," Judson said. "Well, most of the time."

"All of the time," the angel said. "Ever after."

Then he pumped his new wings, which creaked rather ominously for a moment, then seemed to expand and grow into themselves as if they and the angel had become melded together. Standing on his tiptoes, the angel raised his arms heavenward and leaped into the air, singing, "*H*a*p*p*i*n*e*s*s*!"

The last they saw of him was when he dipped once toward earth. The skull of the Grateful Dead wing patch winked at them, grinning beatifically. And then the angel was gone.

"*Happiness*," said Courtney with a strange sigh. "I don't feel particularly happy right now. In fact I feel sort of sad. The angel is gone and I miss him."

"An alien," Judson said. "Not an angel. An angel wouldn't have promised us a reward and then backed off."

"Aliens don't have wings," said Maddy.

They never told their parents, or their friends. They knew they would never be believed. But over the next eighty years of their lives—full and varied and interesting lives—the three of them were indeed happy.

Once Judson was interviewed by the *Wall Street Journal* because of one of his important inventions. The interviewer asked, "To what do you credit your enormous success and the success of your sisters?"

"To an angel," Judson said. But he winked when he said it, looking at eighty-seven a lot like the skull on the second angel wing, all bone and a mile-wide grin. "An angel."

I was looking out of the window, waiting for inspiration. My writing room has a wonderful big window that overlooks a field. Sometimes I see a fox crossing carefully between farmed ridges. Sometimes a rabbit hops nervously by. Sometimes a solitary cat prowls.

This time I was gazing up at the sky. And there were those shirred clouds, like angel's wings.

The poem began.

Thinking of Angels

The clouds float white winged,
Wispy, shirred,
As if an angel
With a silver needle
Basted feathers onto the blue.

        If you are quiet
You can hear her singing
As she sews:
"Oh, carry me away,
Beyond the Jordan . . ."
Her voice lifts like a lark's
And we are carried heavenward,
Where the wind puts the wings
To our shoulders

          up into the light.
          up
That we may fly up

I was visiting publishers in New York City when the opening line to this story came to me. It rang in my ears. I simply had to write the story to find out what happened.

Like Jesse in the story, I lived on Ninety-sixth and Central Park West as a child. And like Jesse I moved to Connecticut, though that occurred when I was a teenager. New Yorkers are so blasé about startling events, I can imagine that even an angel in Central Park would not faze them. Even if they believed.

Wrestling with Angels

My father wrestled with an angel and, like Jacob in the Bible, was lamed in the match. It happened on Ninety-sixth, across the street from our building. I was just a little boy then, in a stroller, but I know the story is true. My father limped ever after.

But the angel is not the hero of my father's story. Not at all.

And maybe my father isn't, either.

He had been taking me out for some fresh air, if you can call what New York City has fresh. Or air. My mom was pregnant and having a difficult time coping with my noisy enthusiasms. So my father had promised to give her time for a much-needed nap.

We had just crossed the street into Central Park, and he was pushing the stroller along a path that winds past a small outcropping of rocks, when something large and dark fell from the sky.

My father's first thought was that the thing was a kite. Or a large bird. Or a piece of metal that had fallen off a plane heading for La Guardia Airport.

"Jeez, Jesse," he said to me.

I saw it, too, and reached out my hand for it. "Mine!" I said, as I said about everything in those days.

But the falling thing was heading straight toward a child playing ball on the grass.

Dad let go of my stroller and took off running toward the child. He was a New York cop in those days, and he had quick instincts.

He was fast, too, pushing the kid aside and out of harm's way. The big falling thing hit him instead, wrapping itself around him. It was only then that he realized that he had hold of an angel.

The angel was man-shaped, the color of old gold, with dark, almond-shaped eyes. Its wingspread was enormous. Dad often said that without those wings, he could have beaten the angel in that first fall—because though it was his size, it seemed to weigh very little, as if its bones were as hollow as a bird's. But those wings, Dad said, made up for its lack of weight. They simply wrapped around Dad's shoulders and head, nearly suffocating him.

All the while it wrestled with him, the angel sang. Dad said that it was years before he realized the angel had been singing a Te Deum. He didn't recognize it until he returned to the Mother Church.

How long the two of them struggled, Dad didn't know. But some-where along the way, the angel got hold of his thigh and yanked hard, pulling it out of joint. A hold they teach in angel school, I guess, because it's the same one that's in the Bible, Genesis 32:25. I looked it up.

Dad screamed—a sound I hope never to hear again—and fell to the ground; but he took hold of the angel around the waist and carried it down with him. The minute the angel touched the ground, it screamed back, as if the very earth had wounded it.

". . . !" the angel cried in some unknown tongue.

"You're under arrest, damn you," Dad said. Even though he was not on duty, he carried handcuffs with him. Somehow he managed to cuff the angel's wrists behind; maybe—or so I am guessing—because Dad's curse had weakened it sufficiently. Or because, like the fairies in the old tales, its power was drained by metal.

Grabbing the angel's shoulder with one hand and pushing my stroller with the other, Dad took the angel down to the police station to book it. He limped painfully all the way.

"Mine!" I said, reaching out for the angel. It turned its dark eyes on me and I cried and looked away.

No one at the station could see the angel's wings. No one in the park had seen the angel falling toward the child. In fact, no one could even *find* the child, though they went door-to-door asking.

Some of the cops thought Dad had booked a very thin and very old man who spoke no English and looked perfectly harmless. Chinese, probably, they thought, looking away from the almond eyes. And no matter how much Dad begged them, they wouldn't weigh him.

"Jeez, Bernulli," the sergeant said to Dad, "of course he weighs nothing. He's just skin and bones. Comes from eating only rice."

The desk officer was sure Dad had been drinking. Dad had been known to throw back a beer or two on duty; he'd been reprimanded more than once. He and Mom argued about it all the time. I remember *those* fights vividly.

The cops finally had to let the angel go because there was no evidence. The angel disappeared right outside the door to the station. "Went to Chinatown," the sergeant said.

When Dad pointed skyward, his buddies laughed at him. He became the joke of the station. "Wrestling Jake," they called him. And sometimes, "Wings Bernulli."

Because of his bad leg, Dad was retired from the force within a few months, and then he really *did* start drinking. He saw angels everywhere after that. And imps and little pink elephants as well.

As for Mom, she had not been amused when he'd called her from the station to come and get me that day. It was a "last straw," she said. Though the real last straw didn't happen till five years later; that's when they got divorced.

I saw Dad as often as I could. He lived only a few blocks away, after all. But it was never very pleasant, what with his drinking. He wasn't a mean drunk, just a sloppy one. And he talked endlessly about angels.

No one took him seriously, of course, though every once in a while Mom would threaten to have him put away. But she couldn't do it. Not legally, not without his permission, since they were no longer married.

"I'm not so crazy as that, Jesse," he used to say to me. "You saw the angel, too. Don't you remember? Just a little?"

But all I remembered of that angel was in my dreams: a dark shadowy figure falling like a bird of prey from the sky in a sharp, perilous stoop. So I never really believed my dad's story. I mean—who could?

And then, quite suddenly, he quit drinking in a noisy conversion that included a baptism and a church where they did laying-on of hands. He changed his name to Israel because, he told me, it means "wrestles with angels."

The new name, the new church, didn't stop him from gabbing endlessly about angels. But these people liked his stories. If anything, he told more stories until, at last, he seemed to have talked himself out. Then he left that church and went back to Saint Mary's. Mom used to see him there at early Mass, and they would smile at one another, she said. Not old enemies any longer, but not exactly old friends, either. That was where he heard the Te Deum and mentioned it to me, not to prove anything (as if after all these years it could have been called proof), but just as if some curious itch had finally been scratched.

Then one night he was on the back porch of my house in Connecticut, where he'd come for a weekend. We were talking, reminiscing really. About the days when we had been a family on Ninety-sixth Street. Dad and Mom; my sister, Jeanie; and me.

I said, "Did you ever find out what it was that made you think that old Chinese man was an angel?"

"I drank a lot in those days, Jesse," he said. "I don't do that anymore." He said it like an apology. Like a prayer.

The air was suddenly heavy. Fireflies seemed to hang motionless between the porch and the back garden. Inside the house, where my kids were watching a program about dinosaurs, I could hear the TV; and from the kitchen, where my wife was putting the finishing touches on my father's seventy-second birthday cake, came the sounds of the mixer.

Suddenly something large and dark, like a meteorite, fell across the moon and down, down, down toward earth. Dad reached his arms up as if welcoming an old friend, and the angel's enormous golden wings enfolded him.

Dark fathomless eyes stared into mine for a second, just as they had so many years ago. And then the Angel of Death took Dad away, leaving only the husk of his body and a single wing feather behind.

Sometimes a poem comes one phrase at a time, as if the mind can only hold a metaphor singly. And sometimes—as in this poem—the entire thing seems to leap onto the page. I heard the opening and, as if it were a song I already knew, the rest followed.

I think it is a poem about the making of poems, really.

Angel Feather

One gold feather.
One gold feather falls.
One gold feather falls out of the sky
And I—
Touching it—
Can suddenly fly.

In medieval times, one of the questions philosophers debated was how many angels could dance on the head of a pin. They wrote learned volumes on the issue. Today the question simply means a silly or fruitless argument.

Over the years I have tried several poems about angels on pins, but this is the first one I ever finished. I worked on it in Scotland one beautiful sunny August day when I really would have preferred being out in the garden. When I finished it to my satisfaction, I headed out to the sun to contemplate bees dancing on the lavender bush instead.

On the Head of a Pin

See this pin, the top a spot of silver
Where a host of angels quickstep
Across the polished floor.
How many, you ask? They move too fast
For a simple accounting.
As many, I suppose, as God's utterances,
As populous as the starry sky.
Still there is room for more.
Shall we dance?